greek
philosophy

49A Stournari str 106 82 Athens, Greece
www.ekdoseis-papasotiriou.gr

| Copyright © | Papasotiriou Publishing |
| July 2018 | Helen Gagatsiu |

Concept:	Helen Gagatsiu
Literary Editors:	Nikolaos Papadimitriou
Managing Editor:	Spiridoula Nika
Desktop Publishing:	Olga Kodoni

ISBN 978-960-491-104-2

All rights reserved. No part of this publication may be reproduced in any manner,stored in a retrieval system, or transmitted in any form or by any means, without the prior written permission of the copyright owners, except in the context of reviews. The moral right of the author has been asserted.

All photographic material is used under the Creative Commons license.

Helen Gagatsiu

greek
philosophy

| Surprisingly Modern Wisdom
| From Ancient Greeks

Papasotiriou
Publishing

ATHENS 2018

This book is dedicated to my brother, Demetrios,
whose ways remind a little bit of Socrates
and much more of Aristophanes.

Author's Note

Philosophy, said Plato, begins with wonder. Philosophy, said Aristotle, is men's struggle to defeat their ignorance. And almost two and a half thousand years later, philosophy, said the philosopher and mathematician Alfred North Whitehead, consists of a series of footnotes to Plato.

In less than seven centuries, the ancient Greeks invented epic, elegy, lyric, tragedy, democracy, political and economic science, history, geography, physics, biology, and, most importantly, philosophy. For the first time in history, philosophy and rational thought emerged from the mythological dream-world, freeing the human spirit and triggering a cultural evolution which, within the next two thousand years, would transform humankind more radically than the previous two hundred thousand had done.

A stupendous feat, indeed, for a minuscule *ethnos* whose most brilliant state, Attica, was no bigger than a New York's suburb, or an English province, with a free population of perhaps 160,000 (including children).

But, I have the honor to belong to this, still minuscule ethnos, so any further dithyrambs might be taken as biased. Therefore, I refer you to the words of the great philosopher and historian Will Durant:

"Greek civilization is alive; it moves in every breath of mind that we breathe and so much of it remains, that none of us could absorb it all in one lifetime. We know its defects—its insane and pitiless wars, its stagnate slavery, its subjection of woman, its lack of moral restraint, its corrupt individualism, its tragic failure to unite liberty with order and peace. But those who cherish freedom, reason, and beauty will not linger over these blemishes. They will hear behind the turmoil of political history the voices of Solon and Socrates, of Plato and Euripides, of Phidias and Praxiteles, of Epicurus and Archimedes; they will be grateful for the existence of such men and will seek their company across alien centuries. They will think of Greece as the bright morning of that Western civilization which, with all its kindred faults, is our nourishment and our life."

The sole purpose of this little book is to provide small, juicy bits and snapshots of the Greek philosophic thought, that remain as pertinent and well-timed as ever. There is a vast literature on the subject, from a plentitude of scholars. I hope that this small anthology will inspire you enough, so as to seek more, as lovers of wisdom, the true meaning of the word *philosophy*.

May, 2016
Helen Gagatsiu

’Ορθῶς δ’ ἔχει
καὶ τὸ καλεῖσθαι
τὴν φιλοσοφίαν
ἐπιστήμην
τῆς ἀληθείας.

It is rightly said that philosophy is the science which considers truth.

ARISTOTLE

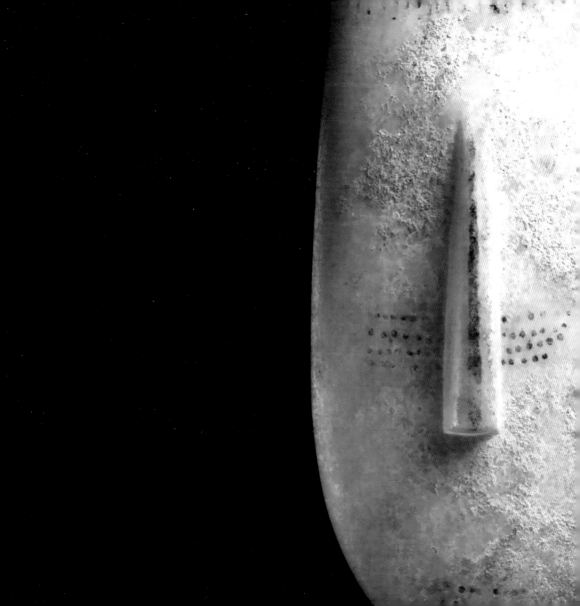

Τί πρῶτόν ἐστιν ἔργον τοῦ φιλοσοφοῦντος;
Ἀποβαλεῖν οἴησιν· ἀμήχανον γάρ, ἅ τις εἰδέναι
οἴεται, ταῦτα ἄρξασθαι μανθάνειν.

What is the first business of one who practices philosophy?
To get rid of self-conceit. For it is impossible for anyone
to begin to learn that which he thinks he already knows.

EPICTETUS

Ἐγὼ δὲ οὐδὲν ἐπίσταμαι πλέον
πλὴν βραχέος, ὅσον λόγον παρ᾽ ἑτέρου
σοφοῦ λαβεῖν καὶ ἀποδέξασθαι μετρίως.

I myself know nothing, except just a little,
enough to extract an argument from another
man who is wise and to receive it fairly.

SOCRATES

Μάλα γὰρ φιλοσόφου τοῦτο
τὸ πάθος, τὸ θαυμάζειν· οὐ γὰρ
ἄλλη ἀρχὴ φιλοσοφίας ἢ αὕτη.

The feeling of wonder is the mark
of the philosopher, for all philosophy
has its origins in wonder.

———
PLATO

Τί περιγέγονεν ἐκ φιλοσοφίας;
Τό δύνασθαι ἐαυτῶ ὁμιλεῖν.

Why pursuing philosophy? To be able to talk to myself.

———
ANTISTHENES

Διὰ γὰρ τὸ θαυμάζειν οἱ ἄνθρωποι
ἤρξαντο φιλοσοφεῖν. Ἐξ ἀρχῆς μὲν
τὰ πρόχειρα τῶν ἀτόπων θαυμάσαντες,
προϊόντες καὶ περὶ τῶν μειζόνων
διαπορήσαντες, οἷον καὶ περὶ τῆς
τοῦ παντὸς γενέσεως. Ὁ δ᾽ ἀπορῶν
καὶ θαυμάζων οἴεται ἀγνοεῖν· ὥστ᾽ εἴπερ
διὰ τὸ φεύγειν τὴν ἄγνοιαν ἐφιλοσόφησαν.

It is owing to their wonder that men began and continue
to philosophize. First, they wondered at trivial perplexities,
then advanced on greater matters, pondering even about
the genesis of the universe. Now, a man who is puzzled
and wonders thinks himself ignorant; therefore, men
philosophize in order to escape from their ignorance.

ARISTOTLE

Δείξω ὑμῖν νεῦρα φιλοσόφου; Ὄρεξιν ἀναπότευκτον, ἔκκλισιν ἀπερίπτωτον, ὁρμὴν καθήκουσαν, πρόθεσιν ἐπιμελῆ, συγκατάθεσιν ἀπρόπτωτον.

Shall I show you the sinews of a philosopher?
A will undisappointed; evils avoided; powers daily exercised, careful resolutions; unerring decisions.

EPICTETUS

Πειρῶ τῷ μέν σώματι
            εἶναι φιλόπονος,
τή δέ ψυχῇ φιλόσοφος.

Be diligent in affairs of the body and philosopher in the soul.

ISOCRATES

Οὐ προσποιεῖσθαι δεῖ φιλοσοφεῖν
ἀλλ’ ὄντως φιλοσοφεῖν. Οὐ γάρ
προσδεόμεθα τοῦ δοκεῖν ὑγιαίνειν
ἀλλά τοῦ κατ’ ἀλήθειαν ὑγιαίνειν.

Just as you wish to be really, not seemingly
healthy, so you must pursue philosophy
genuinely, not for appearances.

EPICURE

Σοφία
μόνον κτημάτων
ἀθάνατον.

Wisdom is the only immortal property of man.

SIMONIDES OF CEOS

Ὁ ἐντός τῆς ψυχῆς
πρός αὐτήν διάλογος
ἐπωνομάσθη διάνοια.

Mind is the dialogue of the soul with itself.

Εἶναι γὰρ ἓν τὸ συφόν,
ἐπίστασθαι γνώμην, ὁτέη
ἐκυβέρνησε πάντα διὰ πάντων.

For wisdom is this and only:
to know the Word of the Mind,
by which all things are steered
through all things.

HERACLITUS

Πάντες ἄνθρωποι
τοῦ εἰδέναι ὀρέγονται φύσει.

All men, by nature, desire to know.

ARISTOTLE

Πάντα χρήματα ἦν ὁμοῦ.
Εἶτα ὁ νοῦς ἐλθών
    αὐτά διεκόσμησε.

In the beginning, all things were indistinguishable.
Then came mind and organized them.

ANAXAGORAS

Τάχιστον νοῦς,
διὰ παντός γάρ τρέχει.

Mind is the fastest thing in the world;
it transverses everything.

THALES OF MILETUS

Νοῦν ἡγεμόνα ποιοῦ.

Make your mind your sovereign.

DELPHIC MAXIM

Νοῦς ὁρᾶ καί νοῦς ἀκούει.

It is the mind that makes sense
of what you see and hear.

SOLON

Ψυχῆς πείρατα ἰὼν οὐκ ἂν ἐξεύροιο
πᾶσαν ἐπιπορευόμενος ὁδόν·
οὕτω βαθὺν λόγον ἔχει.

Of soul you shall never find boundaries,
not even if you track it on every path;
so deep is its cause.

HERACLITUS

Τὰς μέν πόλεις ἀναθήμασι
τὰς δέ ψυχάς μαθήμασι δεῖ κοσμεῖν.

Cities must be decorated with statues;
souls must be beautified with virtues.

SOCRATES

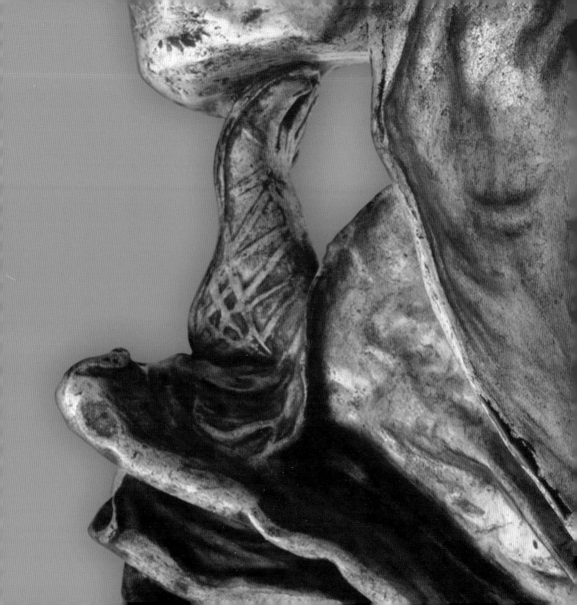

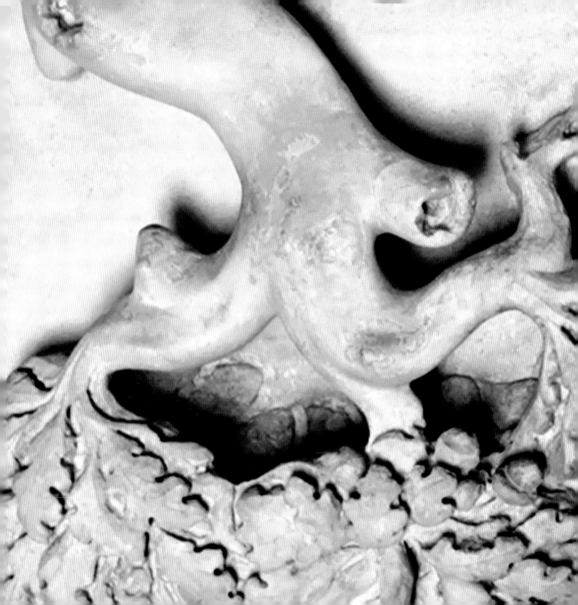

Ἡ μέν τοῦ σώματος ἰσχύς γηράσκει,
ἡ δέ τῆς ψυχῆς ῥώμη ἀγήραστος ἐστίν.

Physical strength diminishes with age,
whereas the power of the soul is ageless.

———————
XENOPHON

Ψυχῆς ἐστί λόγος
ἑαυτὸν αὔξων.

Soul has a capacity of reason
that is ever-increasing.

———————
HERACLITUS

Γίγνεται δέ ἐκ τοῦ φρονεῖν τρία ταῦτα:
βουλεύεσθαι καλῶς (εὖ λογίζεσθαι),
λέγειν ἀναμαρτήτως (εὖ λέγειν)
καί πράττειν ἅ δεῖ.

Three things stem from reason: thinking rightly,
talking truly and acting properly.

DEMOCRITUS

Λόγου γὰρ μέγεθος
οὐ μήκει οὐδ᾽ ὕψει κρίνεται,
ἀλλὰ δόγμασιν.

Reason is not measured by length or height,
but by the resolves of the mind.

EPICTETUS

34

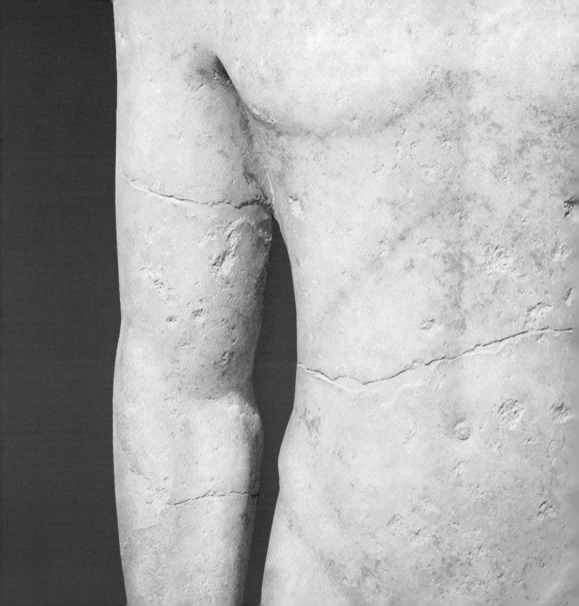

Οὐ γὰρ οἱ πλατεῖς
οὐδ᾽ εὐρύνωτοι
φῶτες ἀσφαλέστατοι,
ἀλλ᾽ οἱ φρονοῦντες
εὖ κρατοῦσι πανταχοῦ.
Κράτιστον χρημάτων εὐβουλία.

Neither the bulky nor the robust in body stand
safe and inerrant, but those who put their brains
to good use. Soundness of mind is the best of all things.

SOPHOCLES

Ἐπιστήμη
ποιητικὴ
εὐδαιμονίας.

Knowledge produces happiness.

Παιδεία εὐτυχοῦσι
μέν ἐστί κόσμος,
ἀτυχοῦσι δέ καταφύγιον.

Education is an ornament
for the prosperous, a refuge
for the unfortunate.

DEMOCRITUS

Ἡ παιδεία, καθάπερ
εὐδαίμων χώρα,
πάντα τ' ἀγαθά φέρει.

Education, like an euphoric land, begets all good things.

SOCRATES

Τὸ μὲν σαφὲς εἰδέναι... δεῖν γὰρ
ἢ μαθεῖν ὅπη ἔχει ἢ εὑρεῖν ἤ,
εἰ ταῦτα ἀδύνατον, τὸν γοῦν
βέλτιστον τῶν ἀνθρωπίνων λόγων
λαβόντα, ἐπὶ τούτου ὀχούμενον
ὥσπερ ἐπὶ σχεδίας κινδυνεύοντα
διαπλεῦσαι τὸν βίον.

As for the true knowledge, it is our duty
to select the best and most dependable theory
that human intelligence can supply, and use it
as a raft to ride the seas of life.

PLATO

Ὥσπερ γάρ τήν μέλιτταν ὀρωμεν
ἐφ᾿ ἄπαντα μέν τά βλαστήματα
καθιζάνουσαν, ἀφ᾿ ἑκάστου δέ τά βέλτιστα
λαμβάνουσαν, οὕτω δεῖ καί τοὺς παιδείας
ὀρεγομένους μηδενός μέν ἀπείρως ἔχειν,
πανταχόθεν δέ τά χρήσιμα συλλέγειν.

Just as the bee visits all plants, taking from
each one its best juice, so those aspiring to culture
and education must acquaint themselves with
all things, but keep only the useful ones.

ISOCRATES

Πολυμαθίη νόον οὐ διδάσκει.

Much learning does not teach understanding or insight.

HERACLITUS

Χρήσιμ᾽ εἰδὼς οὔχ ὁ πολλά εἰδὼς σοφός.

Not he who knows plenty of trivia,
but he who knows substantial things is wise.

AESCHYLUS

Πολυνοίην, οὔ πολυμαθίην ἀϲκέειν χρή.

One should practice much sense, not much learning.

PERIANDER

Ἄμεινον ἐπαιτεῖν ἤ ἀπαίδευτον εἶναι.

Better to be beggar than uneducated.

ARISTIPPUS OF CYRENE

Ἁμαρτίης αἰτίη ἡ ἀμαθίη τοῦ κρέσσονος.

Ignorance of the better is the cause of all evil actions.

DEMOCRITUS

Ἡ γὰρ νοῦ ἐνέργεια ζωή.

The energy of the mind is the essence of life.

ARISTOTLE

Μέγιστον ἀγαθὸν ὂν ἀνθρώπῳ τοῦτο,
ἑκάστης ἡμέρας περὶ ἀρετῆς τοὺς λόγους ποιεῖσθαι
καὶ τῶν ἄλλων περὶ ὧν ὑμεῖς ἐμοῦ ἀκούετε
διαλεγομένου καὶ ἐμαυτὸν καὶ ἄλλους ἐξετάζοντος,
ὁ δὲ ἀνεξέταστος βίος οὐ βιωτὸς ἀνθρώπῳ.

The greatest good of man is daily to converse about virtue,
and all that concerning which you hear me examining myself
and others, for the unexamined life is not worth living.

SOCRATES

Ἄνθρωπος:
  ὁ ἀναθρῶν ἃ ὄπωπε.

Man: the being that reflects and
assays on whatever it lays eyes upon.

PLATO

Ποταμοῖσι τοῖσιν αὐτοῖσιν ἐμβαίνουσιν
ἕτερα καὶ ἕτερα ὕδατα ἐπιρρεῖ...
τά πάντα ρεῖ, μηδέποτε κατά τ' αυτό μένειν.

Ever-newer waters flow on those who step into
the same rivers. All is flux, nothing stays still.

HERACLITUS

Ὁ κόσμος ἀλλοίωσις,
ὁ βίος ὑπόληψις.

The world is in flux, life is
a conception of imagination.

DEMOCRITUS

Κρεῖσσον γὰρ εἰσάπαξ θανεῖν
ἢ τὰς ἀπάσας ἡμέρας πάσχειν κακῶς.

Life and life's sorrows? Once to die
is better than thus to drag sick life.

AESCHYLUS

Μέτρον βίου τό καλόν
οὐ τό τοῦ χρόνου μῆκος.

The value of life is measured
by its goodness, not by its length.

PLUTARCH

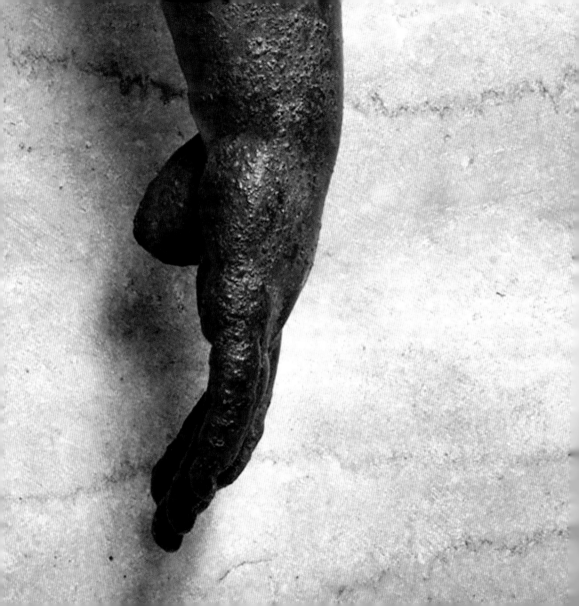

Δηλοῦν ἀνδρὸς ἀρετὴν πρώτη
τε μηνύουσα καὶ τελευταία βεβαιοῦσα
ἡ νῦν τῶνδε καταστροφή.

Death is the true measure of a man's worth;
it may be the first revelation of his virtues,
but is at any rate their final seal.

THOUCIDIDES

Ἦ καλῶς ζῆν ἢ καλῶς τεθνηκέναι
τὸν εὐγενῆ χρή. Πάντ᾽ ἀκήκοας λόγον.

The noble man should either live with honor
or die with honor. That's all there is to be said.

SOPHOCLES

Τὸ φρικωδέστατον οὖν τῶν κακῶν ὁ θάνατος
οὐθὲν πρὸς ἡμᾶς, ἐπειδήπερ ὅταν μὲν ἡμεῖς ὦμεν,
ὁ θάνατος οὐ πάρεστιν, ὅταν δὲ ὁ θάνατος παρῇ,
τόθ᾽ ἡμεῖς οὐκ ἐσμέν. Οὔτε οὖν πρὸς τοὺς ζῶντάς
ἐστιν οὔτε πρὸς τοὺς τετελευτηκότας.

Death, considered the most awful of all evils, is nothing to us;
inasmuch we exist, he is not present; and when he comes,
we do not exist anymore. Thus, death is unsubstantial both
for the living and the dead.

———————

EPICURUS

Ἐκ γαίης γάρ πάντα
καί εἰς γῆν πάντα τελευτᾶ.

All things derive from earth
and to the earth they end.

———————

XENOPHANES

58

Ἐπάμεροι· Τί δέ τις; Τί δ᾽ οὔ τις; Σκιᾶς ὄναρ
ἄνθρωπος. Ἀλλ᾽ ὅταν αἴγλα διόσδοτος ἔλθῃ,
λαμπρὸν φέγγος ἔπεστιν ἀνδρῶν καὶ μείλιχος αἰών.

Creatures of a day! What is a man? What is he not?
A dream of a shadow is our mortal being. But when
there comes to men a gleam of splendour given of Heaven,
then rests on them a light of glory. And blessed are their days.

PINDAR

Οὐθὲν ἔοικε θνητῷ ζῴῳ ζῶν
ἄνθρωπος ἐν ἀθανάτοις ἀγαθοῖς.

Nowhere near looks as mortal, man, invested in immortal qualities.

MENANDER

61

Τοῦ βίου καθάπερ ἀγάλματος
πάντα τά μέρη καλά εἶναι δεῖ.

Like a statue, all aspects
of man's life must be well-formed.

SOCRATES

Μέ τήν ὄψιν
        καλλωπίζου, ἀλλ᾽ ἐν
    τοῖς ἐπιτηδεύμασιν
ἴσθι καλός.

Take care of your good looks, but first
and foremost take care of your good deeds.

PITTACUS OF MYTILENE

Τό κάλλος
παντός ἐπιστολίου
συστατικώτερον.

Beauty is the best reference.

ARISTOTLE

Κάλλος περιμάχητον
μέν ἀλλ' ὀλιγοχρόνιον.

Beauty is covetable, but short-lived.

PLUTARCH

Φιλοκαλοῦμέν τε γὰρ μετ' εὐτελείας
καὶ φιλοσοφοῦμεν ἄνευ μαλακίας·
πλούτῳ τε ἔργου μᾶλλον καιρῷ ἢ λόγου
κόμπῳ χρώμεθα. Καὶ τὰ ἐς ἀρετὴν
ἐνηντιώμεθα τοῖς πολλοῖς· οὐ γὰρ
πάσχοντες εὖ, ἀλλὰ δρῶντες κτώμεθα
τοὺς φίλους. Καὶ μόνοι οὐ τοῦ ξυμφέροντος
μᾶλλον λογισμῷ ἢ τῆς ἐλευθερίας τῷ πιστῷ
ἀδεῶς τινὰ ὠφελοῦμεν.

For we are lovers of the beautiful without extravagance
and we cultivate our minds without becoming fainthearted.
We see wealth as a means to great ends, not as an opportunity
for showing off. In virtue we are equally singular, doing good
and acquiring friends by conferring, not by receiving, favors.
And we, alone, do good to our fellow men, not upon
a calculation of interest, but in the confidence of freedom
and in a frank and fearless spirit.

PERICLES

Ἄνθρωπον ζητῶ.

I seek a human being [worthy of the name].

DIOGENES

Τίς εὐδαίμων; Ὁ τό μέν σῶμα ὑγιής,
τήν δέ ψυχήν εὔπορος, τήν δέ φύσιν εὐπαίδευτος.

Who can be said happy? He who is healthy in the body,
rich in the soul and educated in the mind.

THALES OF MILETUS

Εἰς τελειότητα τοῦ ἀνθρώπου
τρία δεῖ συνδράμειν:
φύσιν, μάθησιν καί ἄσκησιν.

Human perfection lies in these three:
natural disposition, education, culture
and active exercise [of *areté*].

PLATO

Τί ἄριστον;
Τό παρόν εὖ ποιεῖν.

What makes excellence? To turn the
present circumstances to your advantage.

PITTACUS OF MYTILENE

Ὅπου ἄμιλλα
ἐνταῦθα καί νίκη ἔστι.

Where there is competition, there is victory.

ARISTOTLE

Εἷς ἐμοί μύριοι, ἐάν ἄριστος εἰ.

One man is ten thousand to me,
if he be the best.

HERACLITUS

Οὐ γάρ δοκεῖν ἄριστος, ἀλλ' εἶναι θέλει.

Do not desire to appear excellent, but to really be.

AESCHYLUS

Ἀνδρὶ σοφῷ πᾶσα γῆ βατή,
ψυχῆς γὰρ ἀγαθῆς πατρὶς
ὁ ξύμπας κόσμος.

To a wise man, the whole earth
is open; for the native land
of a good soul is the whole earth.

DEMOCRITUS

Οὔχ ὁ τόπος τόν ἄνδρα,
ἀλλ᾽ ὁ ἀνήρ αὐτόν ἔντιμον ποιεῖ.

It is not the land that honors the man,
but the man honors the land.

AGESILAUS, KING OF SPARTA

Ἀνδρῶν γὰρ ἐπιφανῶν πᾶσα γῆ τάφος,
καὶ οὐ στηλῶν μόνον ἐν τῇ οἰκείᾳ
σημαίνει ἐπιγραφή, ἀλλὰ καὶ ἐν
τῇ μὴ προσηκούσῃ ἄγραφος μνήμη
παρ' ἑκάστῳ τῆς γνώμης μᾶλλον ἢ
τοῦ ἔργου ἐνδιαιτᾶται. Οὓς νῦν ὑμεῖς
ζηλώσαντες καὶ τὸ εὔδαιμον
τὸ ἐλεύθερον, τὸ δ' ἐλεύθερον
τὸ εὔψυχον κρίναντες μὴ περιορᾶσθε
τοὺς πολεμικοὺς κινδύνους.

For the tomb of glorious men is the whole earth; they are
commemorated not only by statues and inscriptions, but there dwells
also an unwritten memorial of them, graven not on stone but in the
hearts of men, both in their own country and in foreign lands. Make
them your examples and, esteeming valor to be freedom and freedom
to be happiness, do not decline the perils of war.

PERICLES

Οὐ τό ζῆν περί πλείστου ποιητέον,
ἀλλά τό εὖ ζῆν.

Not mere life, but a good (noble) life,
is to be chiefly valued.

———————

SOCRATES

Τῶν ἀνθρώπων τούς φρονίμους δεῖ
πρότερον τά τῆλε τῶν πραγμάτων
σκοπεῖν, εἰθ' οὕτως αὐτοῖς ἐπιχειρεῖν.

Prudent men look ahead, think out
and prepare before they act.

—————

AESOP

Οὐ μετανοεῖν ἀλλά προνοεῖν
χρῆ τόν ἄνδρα τόν σοφόν.

The wise man must not regret,
but foresee and plan on his actions.

————————————

EPICHARMUS OF KOS

Κράτιστοι δ' ἂν τὴν ψυχὴν
δικαίως κριθεῖεν οἱ τά τε δεινὰ
καὶ ἡδέα σαφέστατα γιγνώσκοντες
καὶ διὰ ταῦτα μὴ ἀποτρεπόμενοι
ἐκ τῶν κινδύνων.

The bravest spirits are those, who best
know the difference between hardship
and pleasure and yet are never tempted
to shrink from danger.

THOUCIDIDES

Πολλὰ τὰ δεινὰ
κοὐδὲν ἀνθρώπου
δεινότερον πέλει.

Numberless are the world's torments, but none more direful than man.

SOPHOCLES

Τό νικᾶν ἑαυτόν πασῶν νικῶν
πρώτη καί ἀρίστη. Τό δέ ἡττᾶσθαι
αὐτόν ὑφ᾽ ἑαυτοῦ, αἴσχιστον καί κάκιστον.

To triumph over yourself is the most glorious
of all victories. To be defeated by yourself
is the most inglorious and disgraceful defeat.

DEMOCRITUS

Τὰς λεωφόρους
μή βαδίζειν.

Follow not open roads and easy paths.

PYTHAGORAS

Πονούντων καί κινδυνευόντων
τά καλά καί μεγάλα ἔργα.

Only through struggling, labor and risk
great accomplishments are realized.

ALEXANDER THE GREAT

Δός μοι πᾶ στῶ
καὶ τᾶν γᾶν κινάσω.

Give me a place to stand on, and I will move the Earth.

ARCHIMEDES

Τὰς μεταβολὰς τῆς τύχης
γενναίως ἐπίστασο φέρειν.

Bravely bear any turn of fortune.

CLEOBULUS

Τί δ' ἂν φοβοῖτ' ἄνθρωπος ᾧ τὰ τῆς τύχης
κρατεῖ, πρόνοια δ' ἐστὶν οὐδενὸς σαφής;
Εἰκῆ κράτιστον ζῆν, ὅπως δύναιτό τις.

Fear? What has a man to do with fear? Chance rules
our lives, and the future is all unknown. Best live as
we may, from day to day.

SOPHOCLES

Ἄνθρωποι τύχης εἴδωλον ἐπλάσαντο, πρόφασιν
ἰδίης ἀβουλοίης. Βαιά γάρ φρονήσει τύχη μάχεται,
τά δέ πλεῖστα ἐν βίω ἐξύνετος ὀξυδερκείη κατιθύνει.

Men have fashioned an image of Chance as an excuse
for their own stupidity. For Chance rarely conflicts
with intelligence, and most things in life can be set
in order by an intelligent sharp-sightedness.

DEMOCRITUS

Μηδέν τῆς τύχης,
ἀλλά πάντα τῆς εὐβουλίας
καί τῆς προνοίας.

Fortune makes nothing; everything depends
on foresight, astuteness and acumen.

PROTAGORAS

Βλάξ ἄνθρωπος ἐπί παντί λόγω ἐπτοῆσθαι φιλεῖ.

The stupid man tends to be defeated by everything.

HERACLITUS

Νηπίοισιν οὐ λόγος, ἀλλά ξυμφορή γίνεται διδάσκαλος.

Misfortune, not logic is the teacher of the fool.

DEMOCRITUS

Τούς μέν κενούς ἀσκούς ἡ πνοή διίστησι, τούς δ᾽ ἀνοήτους, τό οἴημα.

Empty sacks swell with air, fool men swell with arrogance.

SOCRATES

Τούς ἀνθρώπους οὐκ ἐν τῇ οἰκίᾳ τόν πλοῦτον
καί τήν πενίαν ἔχειν, ἀλλ' ἐν ταῖς ψυχαῖς.

Richness and poverty are not to be found
in men's houses, but in their souls.

———————

EMPEDOCLES

Τὸ πένεσθαι οὐχ ὁμολογεῖν
τινὶ αἰσχρόν, ἀλλὰ μὴ
διαφεύγειν ἔργῳ αἴσχιον.

The real disgrace lies not in professing poverty,
but in declining the struggle against it.

———————

THOUCIDIDES

Οὔτ᾽ ἄρα φύσει οὔτε παρὰ
φύσιν ἐγγίνονται αἱ ἀρεταί,
ἀλλὰ πεφυκόσι μὲν ἡμῖν
δέξασθαι αὐτάς, τελειουμένοις
δὲ διὰ τοῦ ἔθους.

Neither by nature, nor contrary to nature do
the virtues (intellectual and moral) arise in us;
rather we are adapted by nature to receive them,
and are made perfect by constantly exercising
them. Excellence, then, is not an act but a habit.

ARISTOTLE

Ἦθος ἀνθρώπω δαίμων.

Man's character is the daemon inside him
[the voice of his conscience].

HERACLITUS

Ἰδιαίτατον δὲ τᾶς τοῦ ἤθεος ἀρετᾶς
ἁ προαίρεσις ἁ ἐν τοῖς καλοῖς...
τὸ γὰρ ἀξίωμα τοῦ ἤθεος
ἁ προαίρεσις σαμαίνει.

The most important characteristic
of the moral virtue is the intent
on good things, because it shows
the quality of character.

THEAGES

Τῆς δ' ἀρετῆς ἱδρῶτα θεοὶ
προπάροιθεν ἔθηκαν ἀθάνατοι,
μακρὸς δὲ καὶ ὄρθιος
οἶμος ἐπ' αὐτήν.

The immortal gods decreed
that struggle is a prerequisite
of virtue, and it is long and
uphill the road that leads to it.

HESIOD

Ἀναφαίρετον ὅπλον ἀρετή.

Virtue is an inalienable weapon.

ANTISTHENES

Οὐκ ἔστιν ἡδέως ζῆν ἄνευ τοῦ φρονίμως
καὶ καλῶς καὶ δικαίως οὐδὲ φρονίμως
καὶ καλῶς καὶ δικαίως ἄνευ τοῦ ἡδέως.

It is impossible to live a pleasant life without living
wisely and well and justly. And it is impossible to live
wisely and well and justly without living a pleasant life.

EPICURUS

Αἱ μὲν ἡδοναὶ θνηταί,
   αἱ δὲ ἀρεταὶ ἀθάνατοι.

Pleasures are but mortal, while virtues are immortal.

PERIANDER

Μή διά φόβον, ἀλλά διά
τό δέον ἀπέχεσθε ἁμαρτημάτων.

One must avoid sinful and unjust
deeds not because of fear, but
because this is the right thing to do.

ZENO OF ELEA

Ὥσπερ τό εὐθύ εὐθέος
        οὐ δεῖται, οὕτως οὐδέ
τό δίκαιον δικαίου.

Just as the straight line does not need the ruler,
so, too, the right thing does not need justice.

EPICTETUS

Ἀρχή ἄνδρα δείκνυσι.

Leadership reveals man's true character.

BIAS OF PRIENE

Τόν ἄρχοντα τριῶν δεῖ μέμνησθαι:
Πρῶτον ὅτι ἀνθρώπων ἄρχει.
Δεύτερον ὅτι κατά νόμους ἄρχει.
Τρίτον ὅτι οὐκ ἀεί ἄρχει.

A leader must always remember
these three: First, that he leads men.
Second, that he leads according to the law.
Third, that he will not lead forever.

AGATHON

Τό διοικεῖν ἐστί προβλέπειν.

To govern is to discern and anticipate.

ALCIBIADES

Τότε τὰς πόλεις ἀπόλλυσθαι,
ὅταν μή δύνωνται τούς φαύλους
ἀπό τῶν σπουδαίων διακρίνειν.

States are doomed when
they are unable to distinguish
the good men from the evil.

ANTISTHENES

Ἄρχεσθαι μαθῶν
    ἄρχειν ἐπιστήσει.

Once you learn how to be ruled, then you will have learned how to rule.

SOLON

Οὐ γὰρ τοῖς ψηφίσμασιν
ἀλλὰ τοῖς ἤθεσιν
καλῶς οἰκεῖσθαι τὰς πόλεις.

Cities are not governed rightly
by the laws, but through
the citizens' moral behavior.

EPICURE

Ἄνδρες πόλις καί οὐ τείχη,
οὐδέ νῆες ἀνδρῶν κεναί.

The power of a state lies in its men,
not in high walls or empty ships.

THOUCIDIDES

Ἐὰν μή, ἦν δ᾽ ἐγώ, ἢ οἱ φιλόσοφοι
βασιλεύσωσιν ἐν ταῖς πόλεσιν ἢ
οἱ βασιλῆς τε νῦν λεγόμενοι καὶ δυνάσται
φιλοσοφήσωσι γνησίως τε καὶ ἱκανῶς,
καὶ τοῦτο εἰς ταὐτὸν συμπέσῃ,
δύναμίς τε πολιτικὴ καὶ φιλοσοφία...
οὐκ ἔστι κακῶν παῦλα... ταῖς πόλεσι,
δοκῶ δ᾽ οὐδὲ τῷ ἀνθρωπίνῳ γένει.

Until philosophers rule as kings, or those who are
now called kings and leading men genuinely and
adequately philosophise, that is, until political power
and philosophy entirely coincide… states will have
no rest from evils nor, I think, will the human race.

PLATO

Picture Credits

The publisher would like to thank the following individuals and organizations for their kind permission to reproduce the images in this book. Every effort has been made to acknowledge the pictures; however, if there are any unintentional omissions we apologize and will, if informed, make corrections in any subsequent editions.

Abbreviations and license information

MET: The Metropolitan Museum of Art, Open Access Policy to Image and Data Resources, in accordance with the Creative Commons Zero license (CC0 1.0 Universal).

GM: The J. Paul Getty Museum, digital images courtesy of the Getty's Open Content Program

Cover Image: Cycladic figurine, Digital image courtesy of the J. Paul Getty Museum's Open Content Program.
p8 Statue of Victory (detail) by Augustus Saint-Gaudens, MET.
p13 Cycladic figurine (detail), GM.
p14 Socrates the philosopher (detail from wall painting), Museum of Ephesus, Efes, Turkey. Wikimedia Commons/User: Pvasiliadis.
p17 Marble Slab with the Recall of Philoctetes, Archaeological Museum of Brauron, Greece. Wikimedia Commons/Source: Ophelia2.
p18 Block from a relief depicting a battle, MET.
p21 Bronze statue of a man (detail), MET.
p22 Wall painting (detail) from Room H of the Villa of P. Fannius Synistor at Boscoreale, Italy, MET.
p25 Statue of Victory (detail) by Augustus Saint-Gaudens, MET.
p26 Small head (detail), LH III B period, Archaeological Museum of Mycenae, Greece. Wikimedia Commons/User: Zde.
p31 Statue of Victory (detail) by Augustus Saint-Gaudens, MET.
p32 Judgement of Paris (detail), Museo Nazionale Romano, Palazzo Altemps, Italy. Wikimedia Commons/Source: Jastrow.
p35 Masterpieces Collection, GM.
p36 Marble statue of a Kouros (detail), MET.
p39 Minoan fresco painting (detail), Knossos Palace, Crete. Flickr/Mediterraneaning
p40 Aulos player, detail from attic lekythos, Museo Archeologico Regionale "Antonio Salinas" di Palermo. Wiki
p43 Kylix painting, Staatliche Antikensammlungen, Germany. Wikimedia Commons/Source: Matthias Kabel.
p44 Masterpieces Collection, GM.

p48 Marble seated harp player (detail), MET.

p5l Judgement of Paris (detail), Museo Nazionale Romano, Palazzo Altemps, Italy. Wikimedia Commons/Source: Jastrow.

p52 Aryballos vase (detail), GM.

p55 Wall painting (detail) from Room H of the Villa of P. Fannius Synistor at Boscoreale, Italy, MET.

p56 Bronze statue of Eros sleeping (detail), MET.

p59 Hermaphrodite sculpture, Louvre. Creative Commons Attribution-Share Alike 3.0/User: Michel Wal.

p60 Apollo holding a kithara, Archaeological Museum of Delphi, Greece. Wikimedia Commons/Source: Fingalo.

p63 Bacchanal: A Faun Teased by Children (detail), MET.

p64 Marble Statue of a Wounded Amazon (detail), MET.

p67 Terracotta figure (detail), MET.

p68 Marble Statue Group of the Three Graces (detail), MET.

p7l Tomb of the Diver (detail), Paestum, Italy. Wikimedia Commons/Source: Dave & Margie Hill/Kleerup.

p72 Hercules and Achelous (detail), MET.

p75 Bronze Statue of an Aristocratic Boy (detail), MET.

p76 Bust of the Philosopher Antisthenes, British Museum. Wikimedia Commons/Source: Allen Watkin.

p79 Masterpieces Collection, GM.

p82 Death of Meleager, detail from a panel of a Roman sarcophagus, Louvre. Wikimedia Commons/Source: Mbzt.

p85 "Diana of Versailles" (detail), Louvre. Wikimedia Commons/Source: Jastrow.

p86 Hercules and Achelous (detail), MET.

p89 Ephebe Narcissus (detail), Louvre. Wikimedia Commons/Source: Marie-Lan Nguyen.

p90 Masterpieces Collection, GM.

p93 Statue of Marsyas (detail), MET.

p94 Marble Seated Harp Player (detail), MET.

p96 Greek Art of the Aegean Islands, MET.

p99 "Thermae boxer", bronze statue. Wikimedia Commons/Source: Jean-Pol Grandmont.

p100 Marble Stele of a Youth and a Little Girl (detail), MET.

p103 Marble Seated Harp Player (detail), MET.

p104 Marble Column from the Temple of Artemis at Sardis (detail), MET.

p106 Príncipe Helenístico, Pallazzo Massimo, Italy. Wikimedia Commons/Source: Miguel Hermoso Cuesta.

p109 Greek Vase Painting (detail), MET.

p110 Bronze Box Mirror (detail), MET.

p113 Achilles by Lycomedes, Louvre. Wikimedia Commons/Source: Jastrow.

p115 Perseus with the Head of Medusa (detail), MET.